UNDERSTANDING THE 4TH INDUSTRIAL REVOLUTION & INNOVATION EASILY

Essays by Tiisetso Maloma

Please take a selfie with the Book Cover and post it on your Social Media. Insert hashtag #BookSelfie

Follow me on Social Media
@tiisetsomaloma

Subscribe to my newsletter on www.tiisetsomaloma.com

COPYRIGHT

UNDERSTANDING THE 4ᵀᴴ INDUSTRIAL REVOLUTION & INNOVATION EASILY

Essays by Tiisetso Maloma

Copyright © 2020 Tiisetso Maloma

All Rights Reserved

Print ISBN: 9798558395655

ePUB eBook ISBN: 9781005505479

Edited by Lara Stander

Published by Maloma Content – www.malomacontent.co.za

Cover, layout, eBook conversion and online distribution by www.bulabuka.co.za

Author website www.tiisetsomaloma.com

This book or any parts thereof may not be reproduced or transmitted in any form or stored in any information retrieval system, by any means, electronic or mechanical, or by photocopying, recording or otherwise – without prior written permission from the author.

BOOKS BY TIISETSO MALOMA

CONTENTS

UNDERSTANDING THE 4TH INDUSTRIAL REVOLUTION & INNOVATION EASILY 1

Copyright 5

Books by Tiisetso Maloma 7

Contents 8

The author, Tiisetso Maloma.. 10

About the book.. 12

Reading the book 13

1. A simple explanation of the Fourth Industrial Revolution 15

2. A timeline of Industrial Revolutions in relation to South Africa 21

3. What is special about the Industrial Revolution? (Extended Industrial Revolution definition part 2) 25

4. Back to Africa and Industrial Revolutions (extended industrial revolution definition part 3)............................ 29

5. Artificial intelligence will turn itself into humans and ultimately will self-destruct 31

6. The Human Greed Pyramid: An illustration of how innovations interrelate with human consumption patterns and natural inclinations, and how to plot innovation that works on humans 37

7. This quick post will make you think you can become a billionaire innovator 57

8. Why man must innovate in his own image as God created him in his own image – innovating per the human greed pyramid 59

9. Learning under quarantine: understanding how innovation works through the Corona Virus and thus be an innovator 71

Endnotes 81

THE AUTHOR, TIISETSO MALOMA

Tiisetso Maloma **authored 7 books – including** *Innovate The Next* **and** *The Anxious Entrepreneur* **– and founded startups in clothing, publishing, events and tech. He has worn hats as an accountant, DJ, web designer, clothing designer, and knowledge trainer.**

Maloma has given lectures at Wits Business School and Johannesburg Business School. He has spoken at various business and entrepreneurship events, and some of which he organised.

His current work involves helping entrepreneurs and intrapreneurs get a leading understanding of the 4IR; and how they can become innovators of novel products. The work marries evolution, innovation, consumer behaviour and entrepreneurship.

Tiisetso developed the EBC Business Model and The Human Greed Pyramid.

Tiisetso's other books include *Forget the Business Plan Use this Short Model*, *Township Biz Fastrack*, *Township Biz Adjacent*, *Understanding the 4th Industrial Revolution & Innovation Easily* and *Tales of an African Entrepreneur*.

Maloma's founded and co-founded startups include Maloma Content Publishers, Bula Buka, Rural Joss Clothing, Startup Picnic, Gabble Heights Clothing, www.goodmorningsa.co.za, eKhaya Moji, Bhovas & Sam Clothing, Defuse Anxiety, and PsychHero Consulting.

He is an advisor at Atimeme App and was an advisor at Pro Hangout dating app (which has closed down).

Tiisetso has worked with Standard Bank, The Innovation Hub, Sappi, ABSA, The Hope Factory, Transnet Matlafatso Centre, Ndalo Media and a multitude of companies.

He's been the foremost blogger of entrepreneurship content in South Africa for the last 10 years through his blog www.tiisetsomaloma.com.

Maloma has featured on CNBC, Power FM, Huffington Post, Biz Community, Under 30 CEO (USA), Destiny Man, How We Made It In Africa, Business Report, and many other outlets.

He holds a National Diploma in Accounting, and a Post Graduate Diploma in Criminal Justice & Forensic Investigations, both from the University of Johannesburg.

ABOUT THE BOOK

This book is a collection of easy and playful essays, written by Tiisetso Maloma, explaining the Fourth Industrial Revolution and innovation.

The essays touch on creativity, evolutionary biology, novelty, Adjacent Possible Theory, surrealism and The Human Greed Pyramid.

READING THE BOOK

This book consists of the most effective essays that I have written on my quest to understand innovation and the Fourth Industrial Revolution.

And as they are essays, they stand on their own mostly, and hence some will repeat certain ideas in different forms.

1. A SIMPLE EXPLANATION OF THE FOURTH INDUSTRIAL REVOLUTION

The Fourth Industrial Revolution (abbreviated 4IR, and also called the Digital Revolution and Industry 4.0) is nothing but innovation moving forward, in the manners detailed throughout this book, as it was with all past categories of Industrial Revolutions:

- First Industrial Revolution (breakthrough technologies included mechanisation, water power, steam power)
- Second Industrial Revolution (breakthrough technologies included mass production, assembly lines)
- Third Industrial Revolution (breakthrough technologies included computers and automation).
- Innovation is the stacking of two or more objects or properties to produce more agile tools or products:
- Like combining video and the internet to establish YouTube.
- Utilising wood and geometry to create a wooden chair.
- Using wood, steel and geometry to make a wooden steel chair.

- Or mixing electronics with biology to create a heart/cardiac pacemaker to save lives.

Let's briefly look at a standard definition of the 4IR (on Wikipedia): *The Fourth Industrial Revolution (4IR) is characterized by a fusion of technologies that is blurring the lines between the physical, digital and biological spheres, collectively referred to as cyber-physical systems. It is marked by emerging technology breakthroughs in several fields, including robotics, artificial intelligence, nanotechnology, quantum computing, biotechnology, the Internet of Things, the Industrial Internet of Things (IIoT), decentralized consensus, fifth-generation wireless technologies (5G), additive manufacturing/3D printing and fully autonomous vehicles.*

Simply, it means there have been breakthroughs in various novel fields such as biotechnology, 3D printing and nanotechnology. These breakthroughs are what compelled the recognition of a new Industrial Revolution. The innovations which characterise the 4IR are distinguishable from, and arguably superior to, innovations made in the Third Industrial Revolution, and are thus deserving of a separate identity.

Novel innovation is mixing or stacking up old and/or new innovations together to obtain more variety and agility. The 4IR, as an innovation construct, entails mixing up such ideas and discoveries.

The recent breakthroughs are identified as new innovations. This means that further innovations are possible. The pool of innovation grows constantly with new ideas and breakthrough discoveries.

All components/spheres of innovation in the world are being fused, be it physical, digital or biological; hence the movement is defined as a 'fusion' and 'blurring' of lines.

Let me give you an absurd example of how innovation happens or is made possible

Nanotechnology is a breakthrough. 3D printing is a breakthrough. These two technologies are, or at least seem, very different. Original innovation is about bringing together, and/or inter-stacking, existing innovations and components to bring into being new or improved innovations.

Imagine the possibility of mixing 3D printing with nanotechnology. (A nano is one billionth of a metre, i.e. the measurement metre zoomed into a billion times – it is microscopically tiny). We may be able to produce, and reproduce, something that is able to enter the human body to kill off cancer cells. N.B. This may currently seem impossible and absurd but, although it may not be possible within this (Fourth) Industrial Revolution, it may become viable in another.

The story above is simply to illustrate that an Industrial Revolution is made up of stacking existing innovations to produce newer, more agile innovations. It follows the basic model of creating new-innovation – i.e. stacking innovations. Innovation cannot be created from nothing; it stems from existing components.

A few examples of modern (4IR) Innovation:

Their newness/novelty is rooted in the stacking up of prior innovations:

(a). Smart refrigerators

Source – Wikipedia: The LG Internet Digital DIOS smart refrigerator. It provides information such as inside temperature, the freshness of stored foods, nutrition information and recipes. Other features include a webcam that is used as a scanner and tracks what is inside the refrigerator. In addition, the electricity consumption is half the level of conventional refrigerators.

Smart refrigerators stack-up existing refrigeration engineering, new power-saving technology, camera technology, and other innovations.

(b). Virtual assistants

Source – Wikipedia: Amazon Alexa virtual assistant. It is capable of voice interaction, music playback, making to-do lists, setting alarms, streaming podcasts, playing audiobooks, and providing weather, traffic, sports, and other real-time information, such as news. Alexa can also control several smart devices using itself as a home automation system.

Virtual assistants stack up voice recognition, Wi-Fi, and other innovations.

(c). Cryptocurrencies

Source – Wikipedia: Bitcoin is a cryptocurrency; a form of electronic cash. It is a decentralized digital currency without a central bank or single administrator that can be sent from user to user on the peer-to-peer bitcoin network without the need for intermediaries. Transactions are verified by network nodes through cryptography and recorded in a public distributed ledger called a blockchain.

Cryptocurrency fuses money with blockchain technology, crowdsourcing, and other innovations.

(d). Genetic testing

Source – Wikipedia: 23andMe offers DNA ancestry testing and other health diagnoses.

With just your saliva, predictions can be made about your vulnerability to inherited diseases. If it can be predicted, it can be treated.

Genetic testing fuses microarray chips, data, and other innovations.

In closing

The examples above are a combination, and/or inter-combination, of existing innovations; some new and some old. The whole point is to achieve more up-to-date agility, use, effectiveness and efficiency.

The reason is that human beings have an inherent desire to push innovation further and further. If you don't, someone else out there does. It is a competitive environment.

The rest is for you to brainstorm what new-innovations are possible, and then maybe create them.

A day will come where more breakthroughs emerge and a Fifth Industrial Revolution is named.

2. A TIMELINE OF INDUSTRIAL REVOLUTIONS IN RELATION TO SOUTH AFRICA

The Fourth Industrial Revolution – also known as Industry 4.0 or 4IR – is the first Industrial Revolution that South Africa is experiencing as a free and democratic country.

It does not mean, however, that other economical revolutions did not happen in South Africa, and the rest of Africa, in the past; but I will get to this later.

Please note:-

Because the collective areas of land that now form South Africa were colonised in stages, starting in the Cape by the Dutch and later taken over by the British, I will call it, 'Project Colonise South Africa.' Industrial Revolution dates are estimates – i.e. the beginning, duration and end of any given industrial revolution is marked by when its sequel is named and recognised - and they serve to identify eras of significant revolutionary innovations in the world. Note that, although different researchers have different dates, they do not vary significantly.

A comparative timeline of the Industrial Revolutions and colonised/apartheid South Africa (extended industrial revolution definition part 1)

* The 'c.' before the year means approximately.

First Industrial Revolution (Steam power)

- The First Industrial Revolution began c.1765 – 113 years after the Dutch colonisers arrived in the Cape in 1652. *Project Colonise South Africa* started when ships, owned by the Dutch East India Company[1], under the command of Jan van Riebeeck[2] reached Table Bay in the Cape on the 6th of April 1652.

- In 1795, 30 years into the First Industrial Revolution, Dutch control of the Cape colony ended when the British Empire occupied the area for the first time. The Dutch were again awarded governance of the Cape for a short period between 1803 and 1806 under the Peace of Amiens. In 1806 the British returned to take occupation of the Cape, after losing their colonies in the Americas during the Napoleonic Wars, and retained control until South Africa was granted independence in 1961.

The Second Industrial Revolution (Electrical power)

- The duration of the Second Industrial Revolution was from c.1870 to c.1968.
- Apartheid against native (black) South Africans was formally introduced in 1948 by the National Party when the country became self-governing; although it remained within the confines of the British Commonwealth until 1961.
- Although apartheid was 'formally' introduced, and became policy, in 1948, it does not mean that the colonials did not practice apartheid; each institution is equally guilty of crimes against humanity; it just signifies a change of ownership.
- Later, still within the timeline of the Second Industrial Revolution, Apartheid South Africa became a sovereign state; in 1961 Britain gave them sovereignty and South Africa became a republic.

Third Industrial Revolution (Digital)

- The Third Industrial Revolution, also known as the Digital Revolution, started 8 years into sovereign Apartheid South Africa in c.1969.

Democratic South Africa and the Fourth Industrial Revolution

It is unclear as to exactly when in the 2000's we can pinpoint the start of the Fourth Industrial Revolution but 'we are in it', as I'd jokingly say.

From what I can tell, the first articles about the Fourth Industrial Revolution began to appear on Google in about 2016; but I speak under correction on this.

What can be said for certain is that many people have been tracking the mammoth innovations in the 2000s and realise that an Industrial Revolution is definitely coming – i.e. a Fourth Industrial Revolution.

Nevertheless, as you continue to read I will expand on what a revolution is, within my context, and it should become clearer as to why we have graduated to a new Industrial Revolution.

The 4th Industrial Revolution is indeed happening in times of a Democratic South Africa – making it the first of the four Industrial Revolutions to happen post-colonial, and apartheid, South Africa.

- - - -

This post continues in the next Chapter.

3. WHAT IS SPECIAL ABOUT THE INDUSTRIAL REVOLUTION? (EXTENDED INDUSTRIAL REVOLUTION DEFINITION PART 2)

The word 'revolution' in basic terms means, 'a drastic and far-reaching change in how things are done.' Following on from that; an 'industrial revolution' suggests more specifically a drastic change in how things will be done within industries. Industry in this context could relate to medicine, media, education, sports and even households.

Planet Earth, and the humans who inhabit it, have been going through revolutions throughout history; think about when men discovered how to make and control fire.

Controlling fire was a revolution in that human beings could then cook, or braai, meat at their convenience. As you can imagine, cooked meat is easier to eat than raw meat; imagine the effort that would go into eating raw meat. Our teeth were probably sharper then and more adapted to consuming that kind of diet. It is therefore likely that human teeth evolved to the more rounded teeth we have now, because of dietary changes over the years, i.e. now eating more cooked meals which are easier to chew.

Control of fire led to many other revolutions, e.g. smelting of gold and production of electricity.

Driving revolution is a concept that is unique to humans as it is something that other animals cannot do: i.e. *Innovation*. Human beings have a cognitive ability to 'innovate': i.e. make hard and soft objects, e.g. cars and software applications; like Facebook. To understand innovation is to understand how Industrial Revolutions happen.

Innovation is the fusion of two or more parts. For example; a chair is the fusion of geometric shapes with building materials such as wood, stone, steel or plastic: a wooden chair, a stone chair, a steel chair, a plastic chair. These basic fusions can be expanded on even further: a wooden plastic chair is a combination of wood and plastic and geometric shapes/structures suitable to sit on).

A different example is YouTube; YouTube combines video and the internet. Facebook combines the internet, other software codes, a concept of social media for friends, and many other elements (status like buttons, a status share capability, etc).

Innovation gets busier and faster as more and more things are discovered. Human beings are constantly discovering new things through innovation; someone discovered how to make fabric and fabric was then made into cushions. Cushions were combined with chairs and we now have chairs with fabric-covered cushioning. (Someone discovered materials that make cushioning and others combined it with fabric to create cushions.)

Experimenting with various combinations of things enables innovation and drives further innovation.

As creative beings, we have driven innovation further and further to a point where we now have things like 3D printing, nanotechnology and cryptocurrencies such as Bitcoin. Even these fields can be merged; recently a Pretoria doctor, Professor Mashudu Tshifularo, and his team at the University of Pretoria performed the world's first middle-ear transplant by 3D printing ear bones[3]. This innovation mixes 3D printing with biology and is called Biotechnology.

This (the above paragraph) is what exemplifies the 4th Industrial Revolution, and simplifies it for easier understanding, as the principle definition (below) of 4IR may be a bit difficult for most people to understand.

The main definition of the 4th Industrial Revolution is as follows:

4IR encompasses a fusion of physical, digital and biological technologies: Artificial intelligence, nanotechnology, quantum computing, biotechnology, the Internet of Things, the Industrial Internet of Things (IIoT), decentralized consensus, 5G, 3D printing and autonomous vehicles.

If you compare today to 15 years ago, you will note that there have been many breakthroughs in various fields. Bitcoin was created 13 years ago and it is currently being fused into payment systems on the internet. We have been using 4G mobile communication technologies since around 2009, and now there is 5G: I guess Bitcoin transactions run faster on 5G.

- - - -

This post continues in the next Chapter.

4. BACK TO AFRICA AND INDUSTRIAL REVOLUTIONS (EXTENDED INDUSTRIAL REVOLUTION DEFINITION PART 3)

Strong evidence suggests that the control of fire by humans (or homo-sapiens – but I am not getting into the evolutionary explanation of human ancestry) started in Africa plus-minus 2 million years ago[4].

We could therefore say that the 'Fire Industrial Revolution' started in Africa. Fire has been used to aid in the construction of many products that could be traded: e.g. mud pots are solidified in fire.

No one has an exclusive claim on innovation although governments and politicians have historically tried to control innovation and revolutions. In addition, politics may serve to inhibit specific people groups from participating in, or benefitting from, innovation: e.g. slavery, apartheid, colonisation, etc.

Even here in Southern Africa, there were many such industrial operations before colonisation and apartheid.

The Kingdom of Mapungubwe[5] – *a pre-colonial state in Southern Africa (between the borders of what is now South Africa, Zimbabwe and Botswana) that existed for plus-minus 100 years between the years c.1220 and c.1300* – traded gold and ivory with China, India and Egypt.

Many amazing artefacts, dating back to that period, have been found in Mapungubwe and preserved in museums. See examples here https://showme.co.za/pretoria/tourism/mapungubwe-collection-university-of-pretoria/[6]. These are just a few of many examples that show innovation of objects, and systems like trading, are a human phenomenon.

Human beings have been innovating throughout history and revolutionising how things are done (N.B. the more we innovate, the more innovations there are to fuse together to make even more innovations and thus cause revolutions in the way things are done). The faster the speed of innovation, and revolution, increases the more things there are to innovate further and the more people there are who participate in the innovating.

5. ARTIFICIAL INTELLIGENCE WILL TURN ITSELF INTO HUMANS AND ULTIMATELY WILL SELF-DESTRUCT

This is a satiric post.

Many people fear that Artificial Intelligence (AI) will one day take over the world – i.e. humans.

Definition of Artificial Intelligence: AI is a field of computer science that makes and aims to make, computers that normally require human intelligence to think like humans, e.g. speech recognition, learning, planning and problem-solving. The scarier definition is: computers that can reason, plan and manipulate.

I even heard Elon Musk[7] share his concerns about this issue and then suggest that governments should look into regulating it.

Of course, AI has and will have many benefits but the negatives should also be considered. People fear AI might be used for nefarious purposes like assassinations of opponents; "Hello politicians…"

The good and the bad of AI

Just for interest, here are three good ways and three bad ways AI is currently being used, but you may skip this and go to the juicy stuff below if you like.

The good

- Self-driving cars: Tesla is the leader here. (Most Humans drive like uncontrollable morons.)
- Assistants like Siri and Alexa. Siri does whatever you want her to do on your iPhone: typing, opening apps, calling Lerato, etc.
- Genetic testing: with just your saliva, predictions can be made about your vulnerabilities to inherited diseases. If it can be predicted it can be treated.

The bad

- Military robots. Or should we just call them killer robots? The US army has them. The Russian army has them. Everyone will want them. Everyone will have them. Including so-called 'terrorists' and assassins.
- One of Uber's self-driving cars ran through a red light[8], in 2016. Shit can't get worse right?

- Faster hacking. AI software that can scan vulnerabilities in people's computers quickly and then hack them.

AI taking over

A possible advantage of AI taking over is it will be able to tell when people are lying and have nefarious intentions.

Maybe the good part of AI taking over is it will chop off the heads of lying-stealing-cheating leaders: in governments, religions, etc.

Maybe AI will conclude that chopping the heads of these people is an opportunity to create jobs and thus hire humans to perform the task. When the humans are done, AI will then simply erase the trauma from their memories.

Should AI take over, it too, like humans, would become over-ambitious.

First, it would become curious as to how and why humans experience certain things and exhibit emotions such as:

- Jealousy
- Sexual climax
- Love
- Procrastination
- Dead-beat carelessness
- Anger
- Happiness
- Drug highs

- Motivation

Then, it would code itself into being able to experience these things.

It will then create males and females. Become homosexual. Become homophobic. It will have sex. Enjoy sex. Be controlled or derailed by the D or P. Become a sex worker. Have kids. Start cheating. Have kids with the side guy/girl. Marry without a pre-nuptial contract. Get fucked over in a divorce settlement. Lose everything. Go to war. Cheat. Become a politician. Become a thief. Crave control of the cognitive consciousness of others. Create doctrines. Create an empire. Pursue wars. Colonize. Colonize planets. Revert to democracy.

Then lastly, after all this, an even more advanced level of cognitive intelligence will take artificial intelligence over.

That AI will become human.

All I hope is that, when AI takes over, it won't destroy the planet like we are currently doing with carbon emissions.

Humans are the manifestation of the emotions listed above already; it is just that we have consciousness. Procrastination is consciousness. AI will get jealous of this consciousness and code it into itself, as well as those other emotions mentioned.

We are AI of the past perhaps. Perhaps, some thousands or millions of years ago, we killed the then-dominant intelligence of the time and took over the earth, because we became cognitively conscious. When you are conscious and possess the cognitive ability to create (animals do not have the cognitive and conscious ability to create a car), you have the ability to take over the world and maybe fuck it up. We have that.

AI has the potential to do that too.

On another cynical note: humans are robots. We are battery-operated robots. We eat in order to recharge.

6. THE HUMAN GREED PYRAMID: AN ILLUSTRATION OF HOW INNOVATIONS INTERRELATE WITH HUMAN CONSUMPTION PATTERNS AND NATURAL INCLINATIONS, AND HOW TO PLOT INNOVATION THAT WORKS ON HUMANS

What if there was a framework to explain the innovation, success, and effectiveness of almost everything? Be it in music, technology, comedy, medicine, entrepreneurship or other creative fields.

This is what I've indulged in for a long while now.

The Adjacent Possible Theory by Stuart A. Kauffman is great in illustrating how innovation forms and ascends.

I've plotted a framework that illustrates how innovation interrelates with human consumption, and how to plot innovation that will work on humans. I call it The Human Greed Pyramid.

First, let's form a frame to understand Success, Effectiveness and Innovation and so set the wheel of understanding what innovation is and how it works

Below, for the sake of understanding, I would like to paint a graphic picture to illustrate the distinction between success, effectiveness and innovation.

When innovation is successful, it means it has touched a point of effectiveness, i.e. a place where innovation collides with the elements that it is supposed to drive and affect.

Examples:
- When a comedian tells a joke and his/her audience laughs, the joke is the innovation. The audience laughing manifests the effectiveness of the joke (the innovation), i.e. the mark the comedian is aiming to hit.

- When a soccer player kicks a ball and scores a goal, the kicking of the ball is the innovation; the ball hitting the net is the effectiveness.
- When an entrepreneur creates a product, if it works to achieve sales beyond break-even point (BEP), it means it is effective, successful and innovative.

Therefore, innovation is that which works, i.e. is effective, and therefore successful.

N.B. I haven't yet said anything about newness (novelty).

Where does newness (novelty) come in when we talk of innovation?

Comedians tell their old jokes to crowds who know the jokes and still laugh. We watch comedy specials we've seen many times and still laugh because the jokes are still effective and therefore successful and innovative (as per the understanding that we've garnered above).

Also, when a comedian performs a new joke and the audience laughs, it is likewise innovation: the joke is effective and thus successful.

A new entrepreneur can make similar products to those of another business. If these new products sell beyond BEP, they are classified as an innovation, i.e. they work and they are effective and thus successful.

Innovation is that which works, i.e. is effective and thus successful.

This is regardless of whether it is new or old. If it works, it is innovative because it is effective and successful.

This is how success, innovation and effectiveness interplay.

I realise that this definition of 'innovative' is contrary to our general understanding of 'innovative', in that an innovative thing has to have newness (novelty) in it, right? That is ok, but please, for this post to effectively provide you with an understanding of that for which we are gathered here today (can I get an Amen?), assume innovation is that which works and is not necessarily just new.

Therefore, in this post, I will refer to innovation that has newness (novelty) as 'new innovation' and innovation that is old (effective) as 'innovation.'

Humans are greedy: Pushing innovation forward

Human beings are greedy. We constantly want to beat the mark and push the boundaries of what has already been innovated. We want to push forward effectiveness, i.e. pushing innovation forward to achieve 'new innovation.'

Everyone wants to create novelties – be it in comedy (Comedians want new jokes, i.e. novel jokes), technology or storytelling, etc.

It has been so since the beginning of man's time on earth. (Or 'Homo sapiens' as evolutionary scientists call us.)

We are a species that can think of an object and build it, then innovate it further unlike our lookalike neighbours, the monkeys, or any other animals as far as we know – from dogs to fish to birds or any other wonders of the animal kind. No animals other than humans have ever built a car.

Human cognitive thought is special in that way – seemingly better than any other animals and maybe even more dangerous.

Imagine what could happen if monkeys learned, and remembered how to use guns. They could – if they decided to – start killing us off. (Why? Because we've been greedily taking away all the land we are meant to share with them and other animals, and keeping it to feed our covetous materialism).

But, they won't learn or pursue that because they are not like us; their cognitive function limits them to just eating bananas, as opposed to making a banana shake with a blender they've invented. They invent absolutely nothing those monkeys, all they do all day is eat food they didn't plant.

Humans build. We created gunpowder, then everything from guns to nuclear bombs and we continue to create more lethal and agile weapons. Our cognition is set up that way, i.e. it allows us to build weapons and then more dangerous weapons, cars and then faster cars, so on and so forth.

We keep pushing forward

We want to keep pushing innovation forward, i.e. cognitively advancing innovation into new innovation.

Can we trace points of innovation and new innovation – i.e. points of effectiveness? Enter, the Adjacent Possible Theory

The Adjacent Possible Theory by Stuart A. Kauffman is effective in explaining the points.

My **Human Greed Pyramid** helps us understand, in a hierarchical sense, the realm, factors, advantages and rules within which we live and are bound by, in order to innovate and produce new innovations:

(a) Nature (including humans), (b) Human Behavioural Inclinations, (c) Functional Cognition, (d) Culture, (e) Enterprising Innovation (f) Novel Innovation and the overlying layer i.e. (g) Creative Cognition.

I will explain The Human Greed Pyramid later.

The Adjacent Possible is a theory coined by theoretical biologist Stuart A. Kauffman to explain and model the evolution of Planet Earth.

The theory states that our planet evolved and continues to evolve as per the order allowed by the environment at any particular time. For a certain novelty to form – e.g. sunflowers (before they were sunflowers), it is dependent, restricted and possible because of existing factors of the present environment.

Here is my interpretation of evolution as I understand it: In order for living organisms to exist (human beings included), billions of years ago atoms broke up and then collided, some connected as they collided and some didn't. Those that connected formed into molecules and the molecules collided and connected to form living organisms. It played, and continues to play, like that until new novelties formed, e.g. sunflowers, human beings, etc.

A Human being (Homo-sapiens) is also a living organism: a formation and combination of organisms. Nature pushed forward to bring a novelty into being; a novelty that became us, just like comedians push to write and test new jokes that they hope will work.

So human beings are an innovation; possibly not a new innovation, since we are believed to have existed in our present (Homo-sapiens) form for anywhere up to 300 000 years, but certainly, our biology is evolving; it adjusts to the ever-changing environment.

The Adjacent Possible Theory has been adopted by other people to explain even man-made innovations. Examples include:

- **Steven Johnson** in his book, *Where Good Ideas Come From*[9]; this is where I first came across the concept and got inspired to pursue it further in my book, *Township Biz Adjacent* [10].
- **Vittorio Loreto** and colleagues, in their research titled, *Waves of Novelties in the Expansion into the Adjacent Possible*[11]'

Illustration of the Adjacent Possible Theory: Explaining new-innovation:

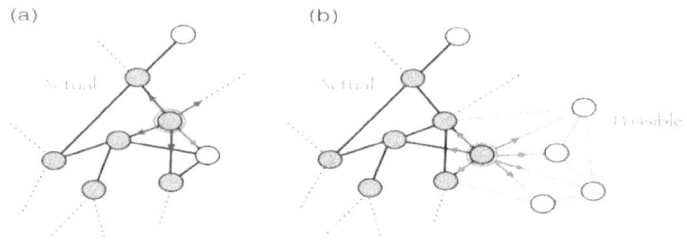

Above: Adjacent Possible illustration

- The shaded circles are actual developments in existence, i.e. innovation that currently exists, or those we can call 'old innovation'.
- The empty circles represent new possible innovations, i.e. The Adjacent Possible. If they work (are effective), they will be new innovations (novelties).
- It proposes that new innovations can only stem from current innovations. The new innovation is possible because of a combination or collision of existing innovations – just like humans were formed from a collision of molecules and organisms.
- E.g. A new music genre (an Adjacent Possible) can only come from connecting actual music tools: If blues music is

new, it takes from, and/or combines, existing elements, i.e. an evolved singing style and the guitar.

- Even jokes are a combination and/or collusion, reflection and/or juxtaposition of more than one thing. It could easily be like saying a phrase and adding a wink to it.
- Example of a joke: - *Q: Why are men's feet on average longer than women's? A: So they can stand further from responsibility.* That's a funny joke I made up. It mixes both genders, adds feet and reflects a societal perception that men run away from parental responsibility.

Let's apply the Adjacent Possible to YouTube

YouTube branding

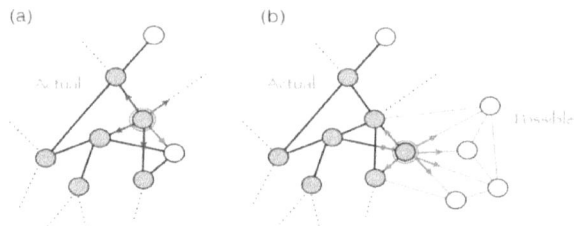

The Adjacent Possible illustration

- YouTube started out in 2005.
- N.B. YouTube had few competitors when it started, the likes of Vimeo and Dailymotion. We could say it fell under a new class of innovation that was online video streaming. It became the alpha of this pack, in that it kicked all the others' asses; the natural selection of the strongest.
- So we will use YouTube as an example, as it has all the correct nuances to explain the Adjacent Possible.
- Before the creation of YouTube, it was only a possibility, i.e. an Adjacent Possible.
- It was founded in 2005, and later <u>the same year, it announced it had reached 100 million video views per day</u>[12].
- By 2005, internet use had grown to about a billion users worldwide: YouTube's 100 million streams per day were within this parameter.

- YouTube operates on the World Wide Web (the web). The web is a platform for YouTube.
- The web (internet for the masses), was created in 1991 and, at that time, no country had more than 1 Internet user per 100 people according to pingdom.com.
- Had YouTube been founded in 1991, it would have failed due to low internet usage. YouTube had to wait for a feasible Adjacent Possible in 2006 to reach 100 million streams per day.

Now, moving on to the innovation of YouTube, i.e. how and why it became effective and a success mechanically: combination/collusion of two properties

- Earlier I mentioned that innovation mixes two or more things.
- YouTube combines two things: video and the internet. Separately, they both have millions of users, even in 2005.
- **YouTube receives success** by mixing two demographics with mass audiences, i.e. internet + video (by 2005 video had millions of users – it gained millions of users through

- the evolution of platforms such as television, cameras, cassettes, DVDs and hard disks).
- The fusing of video and the internet turns video into an agile tool, i.e. availing of free video uploads and stream virtually to anyone in the world with access to the internet.
- A new innovation has a pattern of agility.
- I call it **stacking for agility**, i.e. fusing two or more things; at least one of which has a sizeable following, or usage. Otherwise, it fails, i.e. like YouTube would have failed had it came out in 1991, for the simple reason that there weren't enough users on the internet to attain 100 million streams per day.
- Steven Johnson (author of '[Where Good Ideas Come From](#)'), calls such an innovation 'ahead of its time.'
- From this, we denote that new innovation has to sit on a platform, or at least be derived from a particle with a feasible amount of users. Or else it fails. The other part of the combination can, however, be any size.

The Human Greed Pyramid: An illustration of how innovation interrelates with human consumption patterns, natural inclinations, cognition and culture, and how to plot innovation that will work on humans

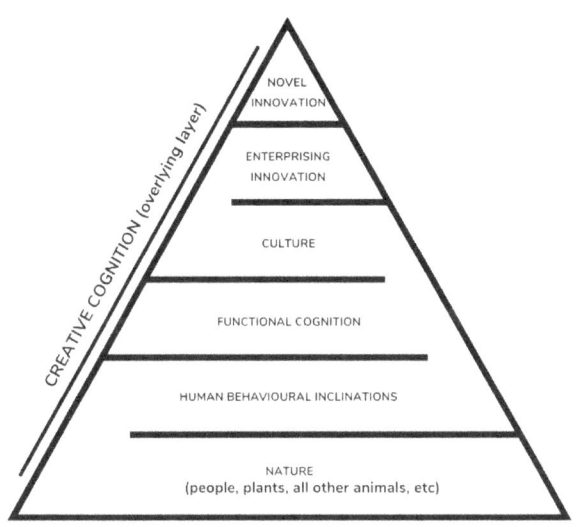

The Human Greed Pyramid by Tiisetso Maloma

Human beings (people) are part of **Nature** (first layer in the pyramid) and thus the subject of the Human Greed Pyramid. They are the main players.

- People have **Human Behavioural Inclinations**. It is where consumption patterns are shaped. It is the evolutionary biology and psychology of the choices we make, either consciously or subconsciously.

- Behaviour in biology (as per biology-online.org) is defined as: *"Behaviour pertains to the (aggregate of) acts or reactions that an organism, an individual or a system produces in response to a particular circumstance. It may be induced by stimuli or inputs from the environment whether internal or external, conscious or subconscious, overt or covert, and voluntary or involuntary. It may be innate. It means it may be based on instinct or natural action (or inaction), originating from inside an organism or a cell. Or, it may be acquired (or learned) based on previous experiences or exposure. Genetic factors seem to affect the behaviour of an individual or organism as well. A subfield in genetics called behavioural genetics examines the role of genetic and environmental factors on the behaviour of animals (including humans)."*

- Crying, laughing, hunger, walking, running, headaches, anger, love, eating etc, are all our **Human Behavioural Inclinations**.

- It is me taking cocaine knowing it is bad for me. It is you judging me badly for it. And it is all the ways a person can view drugs – from positive to negative.

- It drives me to buy drugs. It drives governments to declare war on drugs.

- It is a newborn baby knowing instinctively to suck breast for milk without anyone teaching him. It is conscious and subconscious.
- It is me having discernment, or not.
- All consumer consumption – for food and bad drugs – is driven by Human Behavioural Inclinations.
- **Functional Cognition** is the ability to recognise the utility in bad drugs – even if the high is short-lived. Functional Cognition is how we understand the world and how to get utility from its innovations, i.e. man-made and nature-given.
- As young children, we grew up loving candy, later, we found out that money buys candy. Because we loved and wanted candy, and we then realised that money buys candy, we wanted money so that we could go and buy candy. Even if we did not know the value of money, or even how to count, we wanted money to go buy candy. You could have asked your parents for R10 000 for candy, whereas it only cost R1.
- Functionally, we knew what utility candy serves. And functionally we understood that money's utility is that it buys candy. That is Functional Cognition; it recognised the utility of money and candy.
- If you give a monkey ice cream, it will enjoy it. Monkeys love sweet things. The next time it sees ice cream, it will functionally understand that it is a nice thing. In Cape Town, monkeys steal ice cream and food from people.

Monkeys can functionally understand the utility that ice cream serves. Monkeys and Humans share the same ancestors who loved sugar.

- Although monkeys love ice cream, and functionally they understand and want the utility that it serves, their Functional Cognition does not extend to being able to learn how to make ice cream. Culture is everything humans do, i.e. religion, atheism, eating candy, eating food, consuming bad drugs, etc. Enterprising Innovation is where the leaders and suppliers of culture operate. The priests, business people, government etc.
- Novel Innovation is where new or novel things are introduced, e.g. the first muffin ever, the first car ever.
- A car is made at Novel Innovation for the first time. It is supplied to people at Enterprising Innovation, people understand its utility through their Functional Cognition, their inclinations push them to buy because; e.g. it can get to a loved one (Human Behavioural Inclination).
- A car can get you to work. Thereafter you can buy your children candy.
- A car is made for people with resources from nature, e.g. steel.
- Creative Cognition is those who contribute or control Novel Innovation and Enterprising Innovation to thus get results. It is the entrepreneurs and the priests.

- Successful innovations become Culture, i.e. what people do or consume.
- Successful man-made innovations mirror Human Behavioural Inclinations.

Let's plot the Human Greed Pyramid and the Adjacent Possible and apply it to YouTube

- People crave (Human Behavioural Inclination) entertainment. We've evolved to crave it.
- They then create entertainment utensils at novel innovation via their creative cognition.
- Their creative cognition can create objects that feed inclinations.
- People created video to store moments for entertainment.
- They created the internet.
- These two both had millions of users even before they were fused.
- Innovation is achieved through achieving agility: creating faster and smarter cars.

- It follows a route of mixing more than one property or thing – anything.
- Combining video and the internet is innovation as it creates agility. Video and the internet form an agile virtual tool. This is stacking for agility.
- Video and the internet were huge demographics with millions of users individually. YouTube combined these demographics, hence it is successful.
- This Adjacent Possible of there being video and internet became YouTube, an agile innovation that fuses the two.

Innovation is competitive. Everyone, inadvertently or not, is using a Greed Pyramid to gain a following that hopefully produces results favourable to them, i.e. religious institutions, entrepreneurs, soccer teams, politicians, mining companies, etc. The result could be money, political power, creative superiority, technology, etc.

Newness and the Human Greed Pyramid

It can be argued as to whether YouTube was a new innovation or not. Nevertheless, as I said before, it was possibly new in that it fell within the category of the new innovation that was online video streaming.

Or it may even have been a new innovation in terms of its business model (marketing and location-specific advantages – located in the USA). Businesses, on top of novelty, compete on business models.

Therefore, your cause or venture could be an old innovation, but is new and powerful in how it is marketed or modelled, or it may have an advantage because of its location.

How can you use the Human Greed Pyramid?

- You can use it to brainstorm or test a cause, product, idea or campaign – be it entrepreneurial or otherwise.
- Check how an idea or product touches or mirrors inclinations, and devise how further to twist it to mirror/suit the inclinations.
- Test the innovation of an idea and if it will affect culture, i.e. dominate and/or become part of the culture. Are you stacking for agility? Does one of the properties or combinations *stacked for agility* have a massive user base already? Successful innovations become a culture, as has video and YouTube. With the help of this pyramid, you can think it through.

- Is it an old **innovation** or a new one? I.e. is it effective? Is it **stacking for agility**?
- Of course, all this is Creative **Cognition** at play. What you think (innovate), i.e. your cognitive Adjacent Possible, is the stacking up of your knowledge, experience and networks.
- Where are you getting the material (nature) for your product? Has it already been made?
- Happy thinking.

The Fourth Industrial Revolution

The 'Fourth Industrial Revolution' (abbreviated 4IR or also called Digital Revolution) is nothing but innovation moving forward in the manners detailed throughout this post. It also applies to all of the previously defined Industrial Revolution categories: First Industrial Revolution (mechanisation, water power and steam power), Second Industrial Revolution (mass production, assembly lines) and Third Industrial Revolution (computers and automation).

It is the stacking of two or more properties to produce more agile tools or products. Like YouTube mixed video and the internet to produce virtual video, the Fourth Industrial Revolution carries that forward, i.e. fusing today's technology or innovations to produce other new innovations.

7. THIS QUICK POST WILL MAKE YOU THINK YOU CAN BECOME A BILLIONAIRE INNOVATOR

The following excludes stealing money, e.g. as a government official, to become a billionaire.

How many people do you think watched videos in 2000 by means of cassettes and discs?

Millions, right? Yes!

How many people used the internet in 2000?

Millions, right? Yes! In fact, the figure was about a billion people.

So, if you had come up with the idea to mix internet and video, you could have been the one who created online video streaming. Perhaps you could have been the one who created the innovation that is YouTube back in 2005, and became a billionaire. Maybe, neh?

Video streaming (e.g. YouTube) became this convenient and agile tool for people to watch and share videos online, without the burden of cassette tapes and DVDs.

Some of the millions of internet users and video watchers were now attracted to the phenomenon of watching videos online: millions of them.

YouTube, founded in 2005, had over 100 million video views a day by the end of 2006[13]. The numbers come from the above two places (video watchers and internet users).

This is how you become a billionaire.

You spot two or more services or products (e.g. internet and video), either one, or all, of which already have a lot of users, and that when mixed together form a new thing (novel) that is more convenient and agile.

Then it will be an in-demand thing or product, by a lot of users (millions hopefully).

You will be the only one making and selling it because you came up with the innovation first.

It is damn hard to think of what items to fuse, but you have to if you want to become a billionaire innovator.

8. WHY MAN MUST INNOVATE IN HIS OWN IMAGE AS GOD CREATED HIM IN HIS OWN IMAGE – INNOVATING PER THE HUMAN GREED PYRAMID

This post uses analogy to show why man should innovate in his own image in the same way God created man in His own image.

Please stay with me.

Genesis 1v1 says, *"In the beginning, God created the heavens and the earth."*

Genesis is the first book in the Bible and contains the story of how man was made.

Verse 11 says, *"Then God said, "Let the land produce vegetation: seed-bearing plants and trees on the land that bear fruit with seed in it, according to their various kinds." And it was so."*

Verse 21 says, *"So God created the great creatures of the sea and every living thing with which the water teems and that moves about in it, according to their kinds, and every winged bird according to its kind. And God saw that it was good."*

On the sixth day, Genesis 1v27, "*So God created man in His own image; in the image of God He created him; male and female He created them.*"

Verse 28 continues, "*God blessed them and said to them, "Be fruitful and increase in number; fill the earth and subdue it. Rule over the fish in the sea and the birds in the sky and over every living creature that moves on the ground.""*

It could be inferred that God gave man the responsibility and suitable abilities to look after His earth and its creatures. Hence Genesis 1v28 says man will rule over all living creatures.

It could be further stated that the "suitable abilities" is man's cognition. Man can innovate to create man-made products, e.g. cars and computers, which other animals cannot.

Man also has consciousness that enables him to act with discernment. This is maybe the 'free will' referred to in *deliberate (the past, present and future), form memory, gather knowledge, pay attention, learn (though experience and information), compute, apply judgement, reason, decide, problem solve, comprehend, produce language and produce further knowledge*.

In evolutionary biology, cognition falls under behaviour. Behaviour is what all living things (also called organisms) do. Humans have this spectacular cognitive behaviour, described above, and use it to create man-made things like computers (unlike any other living things).

Science (evolutionary biology) says man evolved. It says the first life formed in the first waters of the earth as single-cell organisms and they divided to reproduce. From that, the single-cell organisms evolved and branched out into the different biological categories/kingdoms: animals (humans are part of this category), plants, fungi, protists, archaea and bacteria.

The Bible does not say man evolved but that (Genesis 2v1), *"The LORD God formed the man from the dust of the ground and breathed into his nostrils the breath of life, and the man became a living being."*

There could not have been science when the bible was written; or rather no post-Darwinian science like there is today. From what we can tell, the earliest writings of the bible were jotted down around 1400 BC (1400 years before Christ was born).

Evolutionary thinking only emerged in the 17th century, i.e. thousands of years after the first books of the Bible emerged.

My fascination with the Bible is that it bestows order and moral teachings. Without order, it is an easy guess that chaos and devastation would rule.

Authors of the different books in the Bible were able to metaphysically articulate how the world came into being, without modern science. To quote Genesis 2v7 again: *"Then the Lord God formed a man from the dust of the ground and breathed into his nostrils the breath of life, and the man became a living being."*

Science says we evolved from a single cell ancestor that first formed in the first waters of the earth. Of course those waters had soil.

Imagine 1400 years before the birth of Christ and before Darwinian science, metaphysically saying, that man was made from soil. Although it is not correct according to evolutionary theory, it is plausible and believable. Not to say that the intention was to lie, but that without the science we have today, it was perhaps the most scientific and intelligent conclusion to make. Also, most importantly, it was made to frame order and morality into the world at the time.

To me, this is what theological philosophy is about, i.e. setting the world right through narrating stories of the past that have moral teachings. This is a scientific way to capture the lessons that history has taught us.

Innovating in your image

I am fascinated with the idea that God made man in His image.

I infer that man should innovate in his own image or else his innovations fail. His innovations have to mirror his image.

I said previously that evolutionary biology describes all that living things do as behaviour. Man's behaviour includes the cognition that allows him to innovate.

This behaviour is his image: all that which we do resembles us.

On The Human Greed Pyramid (follow below), I refer to man's behaviour as behavioural inclinations. The Human Greed Pyramid is a model I designed to demonstrate how innovations work on man and culture, and how to innovate. In simpler terms, the pyramid deduces that man-made innovations have to mirror man's inclinations in order to work. I write about it extensively in my 7th book, Innovate The Next.

Crying is one of man's behavioural traits or inclinations. Now, if you made a film that makes the audience cry, that film would be mirroring that audience's behavioural trait/inclination. That film would be successful with those who like watching movies that make them cry. The message, or testimony, that this film makes people cry will spread and then others who like crying will go to watch it. There are plenty of people (millions and maybe billions) who like crying – or rather, who like emotional stories.

Laughing is a human inclination. It is a craving. A comedic film will follow the same patterns to success like the one that makes people cry.

Science says we came into being through evolution. Therefore crying and laughing are evolved behavioural traits/inclinations of Human beings.

Evolutionary science says that Humans evolved a sweet tooth. Our ancestors adapted the consumption of sugary fruits because:

- Sugar gives energy and we need food energy to survive day-to-day.
- Sugary fruits are not poisonous and the bitter ones consist of those that have toxins. It became easy to discern which fruits would kill you and which you could safely eat, i.e. sweet over bitter.
- Therefore man evolved a love of sugar.

Now, since we can innovate, we stumbled (innovations are often discovered by accident, sometimes deliberately) on how to make processed sugar.

Therefore, processed sugar imitates or mirrors our evolved sugar-loving trait/inclination.

From processed sugar, because we innovate further and further, (we have that kind of cognition), we innovated new products containing sugar, e.g. cake, candy, muffins and chocolate. They become successful because they mirrored, or were aligned to, our evolved sugar-loving trait/inclination.

Briefly explaining the Human Greed Pyramid

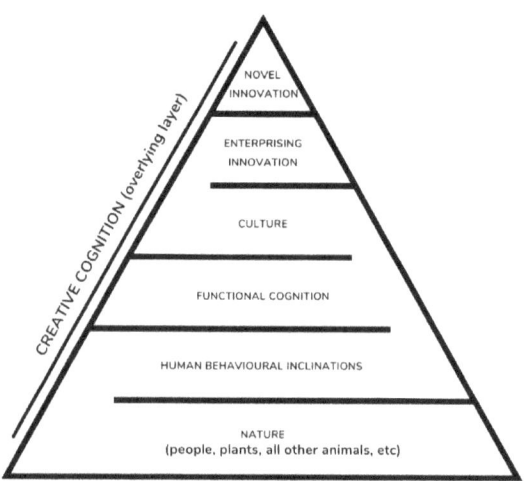

The Human Greed Pyramid by Tiisetso Maloma

The Human Greed Pyramid shows how successful innovations ascend. It illustrates how product success is allowed and or disallowed by human inclinations.

It further shows how novelties are discovered and uncovered through the exploitation of human cognition and man-made innovations.

The pyramid shows how the world is layered from a human perspective, and how others creatively control or contribute to it.

The pyramid comprises 7 layers as explained below:

(i). Nature – (Earth, Humans, and everything of the natural)

This is the world and everything that comes with it, including Humans.

Also, all the products that Humans use are made from nature/Earth's minerals/particles, e.g. steel and wood.

(ii). Human Behavioural Inclinations

These are Human behavioural tendencies. They cry, laugh, have a sweet tooth, love romance, and get addicted to bad drugs.

Their behaviours are both good and bad. Nonetheless, they are all inclinations. They yearn for drugs that are not good for them. But, the drugs give them highs, and it is these highs they continue to chase in order to find the fulfilment they crave and that always eludes them. Colossians 3v5 cautions against bad inclinations by saying, *"Put to death, therefore, whatever belongs to your earthly nature: sexual immorality, impurity, lust, evil desires and greed, which is idolatry."*

This is the bible talking of bad inclinations. We possess good and bad inclinations. In evolutionary terms, they are who we are, however bad or good.

Every product that is out there in use, is successful because at some level it mirrors our natural inclinations, i.e. muffins, porn, Facebook, Mc Donalds, Chicken Licken, etc.

In fact, when we innovate, we are taking chances that our innovation will mirror some human biological inclinations and thus draw people to want to buy it.

(iii). Functional Cognition

This is how Humans understand the world and everything in it.

If they taste that a particular processed product is sweet, e.g. a muffin; because they have evolved and sustained a sweet tooth, they will consume it and want more of it.

Humans understand and get addicted to product innovations (whether they are good or bad) that satisfy their inclinations. They will always want more of them.

For example, porn is a successful cultural phenomenon because it mirrors the biological inclination we call sex.

If a man tries out porn, it arouses him, then boom, he will probably want more of it. That is his Functional Cognition understanding that the product (porn) gives him some utility, i.e. sexual arousal.

Understanding how people think (use their Functional Cognition) is also how marketing plays on people's inclinations. Marketing media products have to be created in such a way that they evoke Human Behavioural Inclinations, e.g. in a way that a person will understand how the product advertised will help add utility to his/her life.

E.g. a sexy lingerie ad invokes in women the idea that they too will be sexy if they wear it. Wanting to be sexy is a psychological yearning or inclination; in the same way as wanting to have wealth.

An advertisement for a new Ferrari invokes in people the psychological inclination to want lots of money. A Ferrari is expensive so (using our Functional Cognition) we understand that driving a Ferrari signifies wealth and status.

(iv). Culture

This is human consumption of the innovations of the world, e.g. sex, porn, ice cream, apples, marriage, movies, religion, heroin.

Both sex and apples are innovations of nature that humans consume.

Marriage and religion are man-made innovations; some might see them as divine innovations. They are innovations nonetheless.

An innovation is that which works and is effective for man, i.e. it gives him utility (either good or bad value). To a sober person like me, Heroin offers a bad benefit, but to someone who is addicted to it, it seems to offer good value.

Marriage and religion offer people value; whatever it may be that they get out of it (e.g. romance, love, a partner, peace). These innovations are successful and form part of Culture.

Widely successful innovations become cultural phenomena.

Culture is everything that people do.

(v). Enterprising Innovation

This is where the world is supplied with existing innovations, e.g. marriage, religion, chairs, cars, etc.

Enterprising Innovation is where people sell innovations they have not invented. They source finance to stock the product and thus market and distribute it to generate cash flow.

(vi). Novel innovation

This is where someone stumbles upon or discovers how to make, something not in existence, e.g. processed sugar.

They are utilising their Creative Cognition.

They can make the processed sugar for mass consumption themselves, or even license it out for manufacture elsewhere.

These inventions can be stolen and copied by enterprising innovators.

This discovery will become successful, e.g. processed sugar, if it mirrors a human inclination, i.e. a craving for sugar (sweet tooth)

Then it becomes a cultural phenomenon.

Novel innovation is how new innovations get added into society. They push civilization forward.

(vii). Creative Cognition

This is the overlaying and layer.

The participants or contributors to Enterprising and Novel innovation operate on Creative Cognition.

They discover the muffin for the first time (Novel Innovation).

They sell muffins (Enterprising Innovation).

It is studying and breaking down the world – all the layers in the pyramid (Nature, Human Behavioural Inclinations, Functional Cognition, Culture, Enterprising Innovation and Novel Innovation), tinkering with it and getting results.

It relates to psychology, biology, religion, banking, physics and all the isms.

It was used by all the kings and queens of history, and by presidents, dictators, entrepreneurs and innovators.

It is operating The Human Greed Pyramid.

- -

The whole point of this article is to illustrate that innovators of any product must consider human behaviour in order to be successful. This is how biology links to the success of product innovations.

This is why man should innovate products and market them in his own image, so they tough Human Behavioural Inclinations.

9. LEARNING UNDER QUARANTINE: UNDERSTANDING HOW INNOVATION WORKS THROUGH THE CORONA VIRUS AND THUS BE AN INNOVATOR

At the point of writing this post, a vaccine for the novel coronavirus (COVID-19) was not found.

It is now well into the lockdown in South Africa necessitated by the coronavirus. Lets' stay safe and follow the recommended precautions.

Scientists around the world are still working tirelessly to find a cure for this virus.

I am not a scientist. I am an entrepreneur and writer and I love breaking down innovation patterns, so I thought, let me get a class in session while many of us are at home in quarantine.

This post teaches how the innovation of man-made things works, and how any one of us can develop a mind for it and thus do it.

It steals a few concepts from my 7th book, titled, *'Innovate The Next.'*

We are going to survive this pandemic.

I will use the coronavirus as an analogy to describe how innovation works, and how we can all have innovative minds.

I am not trying to be insensitive in any way. It's here, we are afraid of it, but let us keep our hopes up that we will beat it. This is the spirit to hold on to.

- - -

This specific coronavirus is called COVID-19. Coronaviruses encompass a group of severe respiratory diseases. It is a novel strain of flu in general terms. Remember SARS? It falls within this family of viruses.

The '19' in COVID-19 signifies that it came about in 2019.

Every year new types of flu come up but are mostly defeated with medicine. Breakouts happen here and there but usually not on a pandemic level.

God save us.

Novelty

COVID-19 (I will call it coronavirus for common simplicity) is novel. Meaning it is new and has not been there before (at least to us humans). Perhaps it existed in other animals (as the claims go), but we will call it novel because humans think that we are the most important species in the animal kingdom.

And there is no hundred percent effective cure or vaccine for it as yet.

Novelty and innovation in biology and man-made things

I will get to how the innovation of man-made things happens. I will start with biology and connect it with man-made innovation at the end.

Humans are a biological innovation. Nature created us. Scientists say that all living things within the biology tree have a common ancestor, i.e. we share the DNA of one ancestor.

The tree of life, AKA biology kingdom, includes animals, plants, fungi, protists, bacteria and archaea.

Let me give a quick rundown of how evolutionary biology says we got here.

The first lives formed in the first waters of the earth. They were a novelty. They were single-cell organisms (bacteria and archaea). They reproduced asexually by dividing: they'd get fatter/bigger and then break into smaller single-cell organisms.

Then later a sort of incest-like convergence happened. They conjugated and started reproducing sexually.

This convergence is what tipped asexual reproduction into sexual reproduction. A new novelty was formed.

This is how multicellular organisms came about (they are a coming together of single-cell organisms). They were a novelty at the beginning of their evolution into being.

Different tipping points of convergence kept happening and the evolution of new species began.

Different tipping points made life branch out into what we understand today as the six kingdoms of life: animals, plants, fungi, protists, bacteria and archaea.

How innovation happens

Innovation happens when things are stacked. The two single-cell organisms converging was the stacking and then new species evolved.

Man-made innovations also happen through the stacking of two or more things. I will get to this shortly.

There is a biological theory by Stuart A. Kauffman called 'The Adjacent Possible.' It says every new development/evolution in biology adjacently gives possibilities to other innovations, and those innovations are dependent on the current environment allowing it.

For example, when the first life formed in the waters of the earth, i.e. single-cell organisms, the unknown possibility (in hindsight) was that these single-cell organisms adjoining would result in the evolution (emergence) of multi-cell organisms.

The earth's environment allowed this to happen. The earth forming through a cosmic bang (go read the Big Bang Theory) in the galaxy 4.6 billion[14] years ago, gave the possibility to the first life on earth, i.e. single-cell organisms.

The earth formed through a cosmic bang and later on it cooled down. The steam from the cooling down and the water from incoming meteorites filled the earth with water and oceans formed.

In 'Science for Dummies' terms, there were chemicals on the land and water, which then mixed to produce the first biological life. 'From non-living matter came living matter.'

The earth's evolving conditions allowed all evolution to take place at various times, i.e. the cooling down steam evolved into oceans, and oceans and land mixed chemicals to form the first life.

To push the point that an environment is an enabler: at one point, before humans, there was not enough oxygen on earth for humans and today's animals to live. By the way, humans are also animals; it is just that we think we are too special to be labelled as animals. HELLO ANIMALS!

Anyway, there was no molecular oxygen for the first 2 billion years of earth's history (21 percent of the air we breathe is made up of molecular oxygen!5). Plants branched out from the centers and added more oxygen to the atmosphere (oxygen is produced by plants via the process of photosynthesis), and so the earth's oxygen levels rose.

Oxygen levels rising gave an adjacent possibility for humans and other animals to form (evolve). We need oxygen at these levels, or we would not have formed, or formed in another form.

We evolved into the human form we have today. The earth's changing environment allowed what was us before to become us as we exist today (Human beings, or Homo sapiens as science labels us). Just like single-cell organisms converged to form multicellular organisms, many other things happened for the evolutionary process to finally produce us and other species.

We came into being through evolution. We share ancestors with monkeys and apes. They are our evolutionary cousins. Say hi to your cousins the next time you see them.

Man-made innovation

Let me first define 'adjacent possible' in simpler, more workable terms.

'Adjacent' in dictionary terms means, nearest in space or, adjoining immediately with intervening space. It already refers to more than one entity because one thing cannot be adjoined.

I said innovation is the stacking of two or more things: like in biological innovation, the first unicellular organisms adjoined to produce multi-cellular organisms.

So, 'adjacent possible' means the possibilities (the 'what can be') created by two or more things that exist next to each other.

I will give examples below that may not be one hundred percent historically correct, but are true enough to bring understanding via the analogies.

A basic chair is formed by stacking a geometric seating shape for humans and hard material. The hard material could be wood, steel or plastic.

I imagine the first chair was created with wood. Then when steel was invented, someone decided to create a steel chair; then came plastic and someone decided to design a plastic chair; then later someone came up with the innovation of making a chair from a mixture of wood, plastic and steel. Still, later another innovator decided that adding cushions to a chair would take the innovation to higher levels. And it did.

Before a seating shape and wood were combined, a chair was an Adjacent Possible innovation. Before steel, a steel chair was an adjacent possible.

All this is possible because of the environment. The earth provides the trees. Plants moving onto land was a change in the environment and the changing environment allowed the possibility of humans.

At all the stages of the different types of chairs first being created, they were novel like COVID-19 is novel today.

To innovate a novel thing, your thinking always has to be, "What I can adjoin to create a novel thing?"

At some stage, a couch was novel because someone created it first. They thought a couch would be something innovative and useful for the human body. And it was.

Someone then created a recliner chair and it too was novel.

Novel innovation is the continual process of adding additional components to existing innovations that gives them the extra efficiency and agility to perform well in different stages of a world that continually changes.

A chair is efficient because it allows humans to sit and rest. It is agile because it is better than sitting on a rock.

Innovation follows efficiency and agility. An MP3 disc is more efficient and agile than an audio CD because it can store more songs. An iPod stores more songs than an MP3 disc and is therefore even more efficient. It is also more agile as it fits easily into a pocket whereas disc players had to be a lot bulkier.

Today we have music streaming which is more efficient and agile than both iPods and disc players. You can stream and play music on your phone, home computer, work computer, on Bluetooth speakers, etc.

Innovation borrows across industries.

At its start, Internet technology was mainly used by the military. Academics borrowed it to create the World Wide Web applications, then, it went mainstream and global. Now the internet is also used for many social activities, streaming music being one of them.

You can take products or technologies used by one industry and fuse them to other industries. 3D printing is now used in biology. Recently a doctor, Professor Mashudu Tshifularo, and his team at the University of Pretoria performed the world's first middle-ear transplant by 3D-printing ear bones. This mixing of 3D printing with biology is called biotechnology.

Biotechnology is the fusing of technology and medical science.

Imagine the adjacent possibilities opened by the creation of the first combustion engine (an engine that burns something, e.g. petrol or coal, to propel a mechanical creation).

- The steam train was invented: It used coal to boil water and produce steam and the steam propelled/agitated pistons to move and thus produce energy to move the train.
- Then someone engineered an engine that uses fuel combustion (petrol or diesel).
- Based on that, someone invented an automobile/car.
- Then a gas-powered lawnmower.
- Then an aeroplane.
- Electricity was an innovation. Then came many other things, e.g. electric lawnmowers. Electric trains. Today we have electric cars.

Being innovative therefore means that one has to have the knowledge and discipline to indulge in a variety of fields. To have invented a chair, you would have had to figure out that a tree could be cut down and then carved into a sitting shape. You would also have to have known which kinds of trees would make the best quality chairs. This is knowledge of the types of trees/wood, carving, and design/aesthetics.

Innovation is the stacking of various things.

The coronavirus could also be a stack of many things. But at the moment its concoction is so novel that it is tough to figure out a cure to curb its spread.

Maybe today's environment (allowing environment) makes it easy for us to be epically affected by viruses: atmospheric pollution, unhealthy eating, reduction of body mobility, too much smoking, etc.

I trust these scientists will find a cure. They did for novel diseases like polio and malaria. They just have to mix and stack this and that, and like the doctor (Professor Mashudu Tshifularo) who performed the world's first middle-ear transplant by borrowing from 3D technology, they also have to borrow from somewhere. They would have to immerse themselves in various disciplines, i.e. studying both human biology as well as the biology of other animals: apparently the coronavirus comes from pangolins.

They will be innovative (the scientist).

You too can be innovative. At this time, you can add to your skill sets. A variety of skills/disciplines and insights into various disciplines allows you to see the future, i.e. the adjacent possible. You can adjoin things. By adjoining them, you become the novel innovator.

Today's environment has so many existing innovations that the Adjacent Possible is greater. It just needs connectors.

In the words of Kendrick Lamar, 'nigga, we gon' be alright.'

God save us all.

ENDNOTES

[1] Dutch East India Company https://en.wikipedia.org/wiki/Dutch_East_India_Company (29 April 2021)

[2] Jan van Riebeeck https://en.wikipedia.org/wiki/Jan_van_Riebeeck (29 April 2021)

[3] UP academic pioneers world's first middle ear transplant using 3D-printed bones https://www.up.ac.za/news/post_2750323-up-academic-pioneers-worlds-first-middle-ear-transplant-using-3d-printed-bones (14 March 2019)

[4] Control of fire by early humans

https://en.wikipedia.org/wiki/Control_of_fire_by_early_humans (29 April 2021)

[5] Kingdoms of southern Africa: Mapungubwe https://www.sahistory.org.za/article/kingdoms-southern-africa-mapungubwe (29 April 2021)

[6] Mapungubwe Collection – University of Pretoria https://showme.co.za/pretoria/tourism/mapungubwe-collection-university-of-pretoria/ (29 April 2021)

[7] Elon Musk says he's terrified of AI taking over the world https://www.businessinsider.co.za/elon-musk-maureen-dowd-ai-google-deepmind-wargames-2020-7 (28 July 2020)

[8] Uber says it's reviewing an incident of their self-driving car running a red light https://www.theverge.com/2016/12/14/13960836/uber-self-driving-car-san-francisco-red-light-safety (14 December 2016)

[9] *Where Good Ideas Come From – The Natural History of Innovation, by Steven Johnson. Where Good Ideas Come from: The Natural History of Innovation:* https://www.goodreads.com/book/show/8034188-where-good-ideas-come-from *(Illustrated Edition, October 4, 2011)*

[10] Township Biz Adjacent http://www.tiisetsomaloma.com/2018/04/20/townships-and-ghettos-are-a-goldmine-favourable-to-young-black-b2c-entrepreneurs-understanding-the-billion-rands-worth-township-economy-through-the-adjacent-possible-theory/ (20 April 2018)

[11] Waves of Novelties in the Expansion into the Adjacent Possible https://journals.plos.org/plosone/article?id=10.1371/journal.pone.0179303 (08 June 2017)

[13] *YouTube hits 100m videos per day* *http://news.bbc.co.uk/2/hi/technology/5186618.stm* (17 July 2006)

[14] Big Bang https://en.wikipedia.org/wiki/Big_Bang (29 April 2021)

[15] The Origin of Oxygen in Earth's Atmosphere

https://www.scientificamerican.com/article/origin-of-oxygen-in-atmosphere/ (19 August 2009)

www.ingramcontent.com/pod-product-compliance
Lightning Source LLC
Chambersburg PA
CBHW070450220526
45466CB00004B/1795